A field guide to Winter

For Julie x – G.D.

For Antoni, Hannah and Emmelie. I hope this book helps
you uncover the magic of winter – D.B.

First published in the United Kingdom in 2025 by
Thames & Hudson Ltd, 6–24 Britannia Street, London WC1X 9JD

A Field Guide to Winter © 2025 Thames & Hudson Ltd, London
Text © 2025 Gabby Dawnay
Illustrations © 2025 Dorien Brouwers

All Rights Reserved. No part of this publication may be reproduced
or transmitted in any form or by any means, electronic or mechanical,
including photocopy, recording or any other information storage and
retrieval system, without prior permission in writing from the publisher.

EU Authorized Representative: Interart S.A.R.L.
19 rue Charles Auray, 93500 Pantin, Paris, France
productsafety@thameshudson.co.uk
interart.fr

A CIP catalogue record for this book is available from the British Library

ISBN 978-0-500-65354-8
01

Printed and bound in China by Toppan Leefung Printing Limited

FSC MIX Paper | Supporting responsible forestry FSC® C104723

Be the first to know about our new releases,
exclusive content and author events by visiting
thamesandhudson.com
thamesandhudsonusa.com
thamesandhudson.com.au

A field guide to Winter

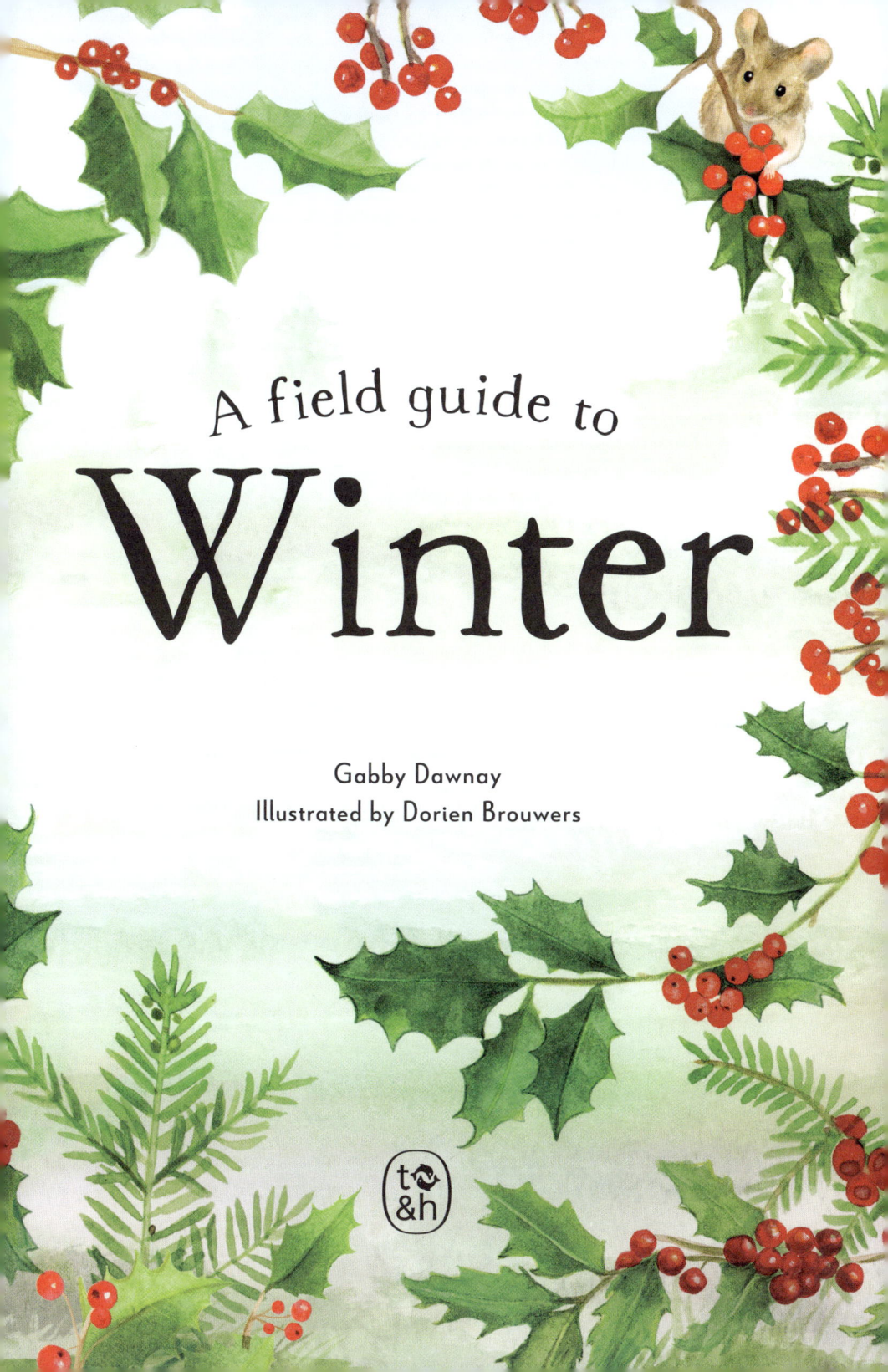

Gabby Dawnay
Illustrated by Dorien Brouwers

what's inside?

6 **Wild by nature**
Welcome to winter

8 **Sensing winter**
Noticing nature's changes

10 **Short days, long nights**
A poem to read by candlelight

12 **What is winter?**
The how and why of the season

14 **Let it snow!**
Where does snow come from?

16 **Footprints in the snow**
How to identify animal tracks

18 **Winter snooze**
Who sleeps through winter?

20 **Once upon a winter's night**
Write a bedtime story for a sleepy bear

22 **Hidden bugs**
Where do all the insects go?

24 **Bare branches**
Why trees lose their leaves

26 **Forever green**
Trees that keep their leaves

28 **Winter leaves**
How to identify evergreen trees

30 **Frozen gems**
Make your own ice ornaments

32 **Freezing Jack Frost**
Chilly winter mornings

34 **Life under the ice**
What happens to pond life?

36	**A warming winter soup** To sip from a mug	50	**Mini night sky** Make your own constellation lantern
38	**Party time for polar bears** A song to sing on a winter walk	52	**Treasure hunt** Searching for signs of winter
40	**Frosty feathers** What do birds do in winter?	54	**Winter's bone** A poem to read on a chilly day
42	**Lending birds a helping hand** How to help birds in winter	56	**Go prepared** Tips for the outdoors
44	**Cold winds blow** Make your own winter wind chimes	58	**Field notes** Recording winter's changes
46	**Starry, starry night** All eyes on the winter skies	60	Winter words
		62	Index
48	**Pictures in the sky** How to identify constellations	64	About the author and illustrator

wild by nature

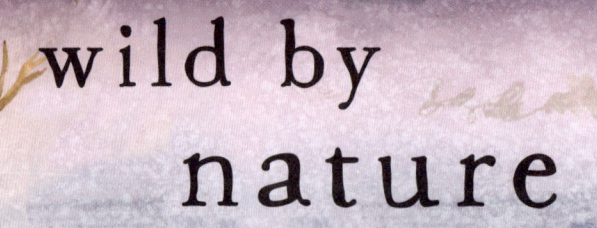

Welcome to winter

Let's learn all about winter by spending time in the wild. Because the more you spend time with nature, the better friends you'll become.

You will find that by being CURIOUS about nature, CREATIVE in nature and KIND to nature you'll quickly become a nature expert. There's so much fun to be had just by playing, talking, asking questions and getting creative in the wild. So what are you waiting for?

HOW TO MAKE NATURE YOUR FRIEND

BE CURIOUS
What questions spring to mind?
What do you know?
What don't you know?
How can you find out more?

BE CREATIVE
Take the time to look closely at nature.
What colours, shapes and patterns do you notice?
What connections can you find?

BE KIND
Imagine the world from a bug's point of view...
... or from a bird's.
How old is this tree and what has it seen?
If you were a flower, would you want to be picked?

LEARN
Discover more about nature.

FEEL
How do you feel in nature?

BE
Be a part of nature.

sensing winter

Noticing nature's changes

The chilly winds of winter blow in. As branches become bare and the ground beneath our feet freezes hard, it's time for us to wrap up warm!

Go for a walk and find a tree that is away from noisy roads and playgrounds. Stand with your back to it.

SMELL — Close your eyes and take a deep breath. What can you smell?

LISTEN — Stand very still and listen to the sounds. What can you hear?

LOOK — Open your eyes slowly, as if you've just woken up. What can you see?

TOUCH — Crouch down and touch the ground. What can you feel?

TASTE — Stretch up to the sky and lick your lips. What can you taste?

Whether you live in a busy city or quiet countryside, you can use your super senses to spot the changes in nature as they happen. Have you noticed any of these signs lately?

THE SIGNS OF WINTER

BARE BRANCHES on many trees

FEWER BIRDS to spot. Many have migrated

ANIMALS slow down and some hibernate

BUGS seem to disappear

PONDS and puddles freeze

FROSTY MORNINGS and sometimes it snows

THE GROUND becomes hard as rock

COLD WEATHER means chilly noses

SHORTEST DAYS and longest nights

short days, long nights

A poem to read by candlelight

When the shadows are long
and stretch into the night...
When the birds stop their song
for they seem to take fright...

When your breath comes in puffs
just as pale as a cloud
and the wind chills your cheeks
till you shout very loud...

'Please stop freezing my nose
and stop blowing my hair.
I am cold to my toes
and it's really not fair!'

But look up at the sky
and you'll see before long
that the stars seem to fly
and the moon has a song...

Then the still of the night
turns the air into snow
and a blanket of white
covers everything so...

Never mind days are short
and the shadows are long
when the wonder of winter
is there all along!

LISTEN What does snow sound like?

LEARN Stay warm by rubbing your hands together, running on the spot and star jumping!

what is winter?

The how and why of the season

Winter is the coldest season, which means it's time to wrap up warm! It is when Earth tilts furthest away from the sun. The temperature drops and the days get shorter as less sunlight reaches us.

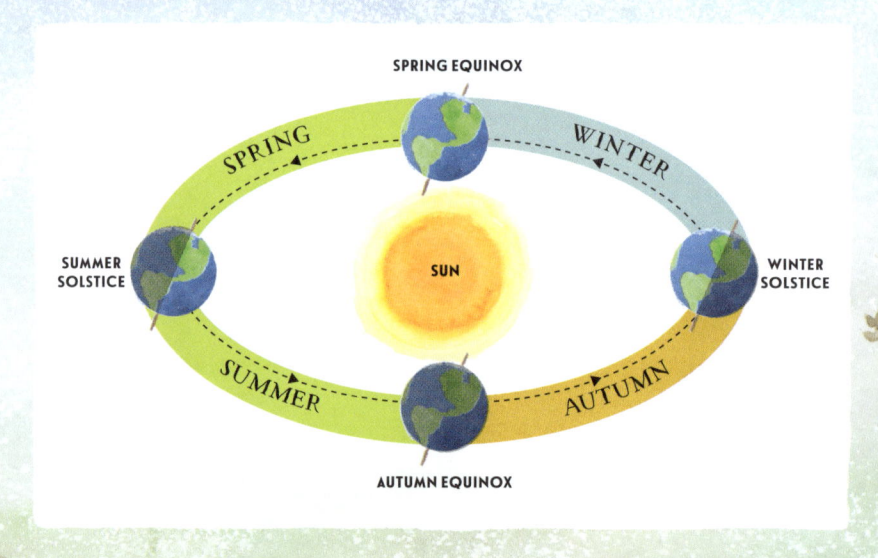

SPRING EQUINOX

SPRING

WINTER

SUMMER SOLSTICE

SUN

WINTER SOLSTICE

SUMMER

AUTUMN

AUTUMN EQUINOX

♥ **FEEL** What signs of winter do you notice? Is it dark when you set out for school?

★ **BE** Imagine you're a rabbit or fox in winter. What would you do to stay warm?

The **winter solstice** is the shortest day and longest night of the year. The date can vary slighty from year to year but happens on or around 21 December in the **northern hemisphere** and on or around 21 June in the **southern hemisphere**.

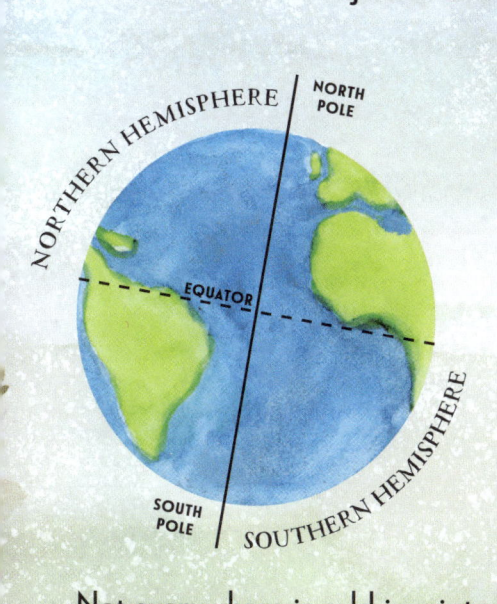

The shorter days and colder weather mean winter is the season when nature slows down. Many plants and animals use these few months to recharge and rest in preparation for the next season – spring.

Not everywhere is cold in winter. Places around the **equator** – the invisible line around Earth's middle – stay warm all year round. But the closer you get to the North or South Pole, the colder it gets in winter.

let it snow!

Where does snow come from?

One cold winter's night, when the pinprick stars are twinkling brighter than bright, something magical is happening in the cold, cold air...

High up in the velvety blue-black sky, tiny ICE CRYSTALS are forming in intricate shapes and beautiful patterns.

Each crystal is unique – no two are the same – but every single one is hexagonal, which means they have six corners or points. What are these extraordinary microscopic sparkles? They are SNOWFLAKES, of course!

These delicate crystals grow and join together until they are heavy enough to fall from the sky as snow.

Snow lands silently in the night, cloaking gardens, parks, pathways and roads in a soft, fluffy, white blanket.

Has it snowed where you live?

LISTEN What sound does the snow make under your feet?

TOUCH Does it feel dry and powdery or wet and slushy?

TASTE Stick out your tongue and catch some snowflakes! What do they taste like?

You wake with a sense that something is different... behind your curtains the snow glows and glistens in the morning sunlight.

With a heart beating with excitement, you pull on your coat and boots and run outside, leaving fresh footprints on the path...

Time to build a SNOWMAN!

footprints in the snow

How to identify animal tracks

DEER
- Deer have cloven hooves, which means they are split down the middle.
- Each half is rounded at the bottom and pointy at the top.
- LOOK-ALIKE: Sheep also have cloven hooves but theirs are less pointy.

FOX
- 4 toes (2 at the front and 1 on each side) and a larger rear **paw pad**
- Visible claw marks
- LOOK-ALIKE: Dog paw prints are similar, but a fox's are usually narrower.

Deer

Sheep

Dog

Fox

> **TIP** *Even if it hasn't snowed, you can look for animal tracks in the mud.*

BIRD
- It's easy to spot bird tracks, but harder to tell what kind of bird made them.
- Most birds have 3 toes that point forward and 1 that points back.
- Water birds – like ducks, geese and gulls – have **webbed feet**.

> 👁 LOOK for other clues:
> What size are the prints?
> How many can you count?
> Where do they lead?

Duck

Robin

Rabbit

RABBIT
- Longer back feet
- Because of the way they jump, the back footprints are normally ahead of the front ones, in a 'Y' shape.
- Rabbits have fluffy feet, so you might not be able to see the individual toes.
- LOOK-ALIKE: Squirrels also have longer back feet, but they are smaller than a rabbit's.

Squirrel

winter snooze

Who sleeps through winter?

During the cold winter months, when there is less food to eat, many creatures go into a sleepy state called **torpor** to help save their energy.

This is when an animal's body temperature drops and its **metabolism** — the process in a body that turns food into energy — slows down. Animals in torpor spend a lot of time resting, but they still get up from time to time.

TOADS, NEWTS and LIZARDS go into torpor and shelter in mud and compost heaps, or under fallen leaves and logs. SNAKES sometimes use old rabbit burrows to snuggle up in. Snoozy BADGERS slow down and spend most of the winter months underground.

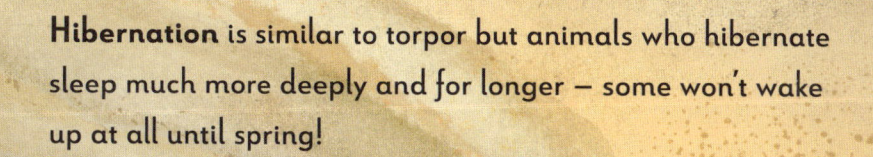

Hibernation is similar to torpor but animals who hibernate sleep much more deeply and for longer — some won't wake up at all until spring!

BEARS are famous hibernators. Before finding a cosy cave or hollow log to hibernate in, they spend months eating as much as possible so they don't get hungry while they snooze.

In the UK, DORMICE, HEDGEHOGS and BATS are the only animals that truly hibernate.

LEARN The shelter where an animal sleeps in winter is called a 'hibernaculum' — isn't that a brilliant word?

once upon a winter's night

Write a bedtime story for a sleepy bear

There's nothing like a story when it's cold and dark outside and you're safe and snug as a bug in bed! Would you like to write your own bedtime story to send a hibernating bear to sleep?

YOU WILL NEED:
- a pen and notebook
- a cosy nook to write in
- a sprinkle of inspiration
- a twinkle of imagination

Start by asking yourself...

WHERE DOES THE STORY BEGIN?

In a wild wood...
On a snow-covered mountain...
A frosty field with a sparkling, frozen lake...

WHAT KIND OF STORY IS IT?

An adventure, full of action and danger?
A 'chilling' story to thrill and delight?
Maybe a mystery that needs to be solved?
Will you invent a fairytale?

WHO IS THE STORY ABOUT?

A fiery dragon who forgets where
he hid a precious jewel...
A fox who must find the ingredients
to make her friend a cake...
A mouse who needs a new winter house...

Will your tale have a happy ending or finish with
a mystery revealed? It's entirely up to you!

Once you are ready, begin
to write your story down. You
can illustrate it too, if you like.
Or just go ahead and speak
it out loud, straight from
your imagination!

hidden bugs

Where do all the insects go?

Listen... can you hear the sound of busy bugs buzzing around? Probably not! Where have they all gone?

Some insects go into a sleepy state – similar to hibernation – called **diapause**, where they stop moving, growing or ageing. It's like they press the pause button on their lives until the weather warms up again!

Bugs that go into diapause wait out the winter in sheltered places. LADYBIRDS huddle together in cracks. Some BUTTERFLIES can be found hanging upside down in sheds or in other nooks and crannies. HONEYBEES hunker down in hives, while SOLITARY BEES seal themselves up in hollow stems – or check in to a cosy bug hotel!

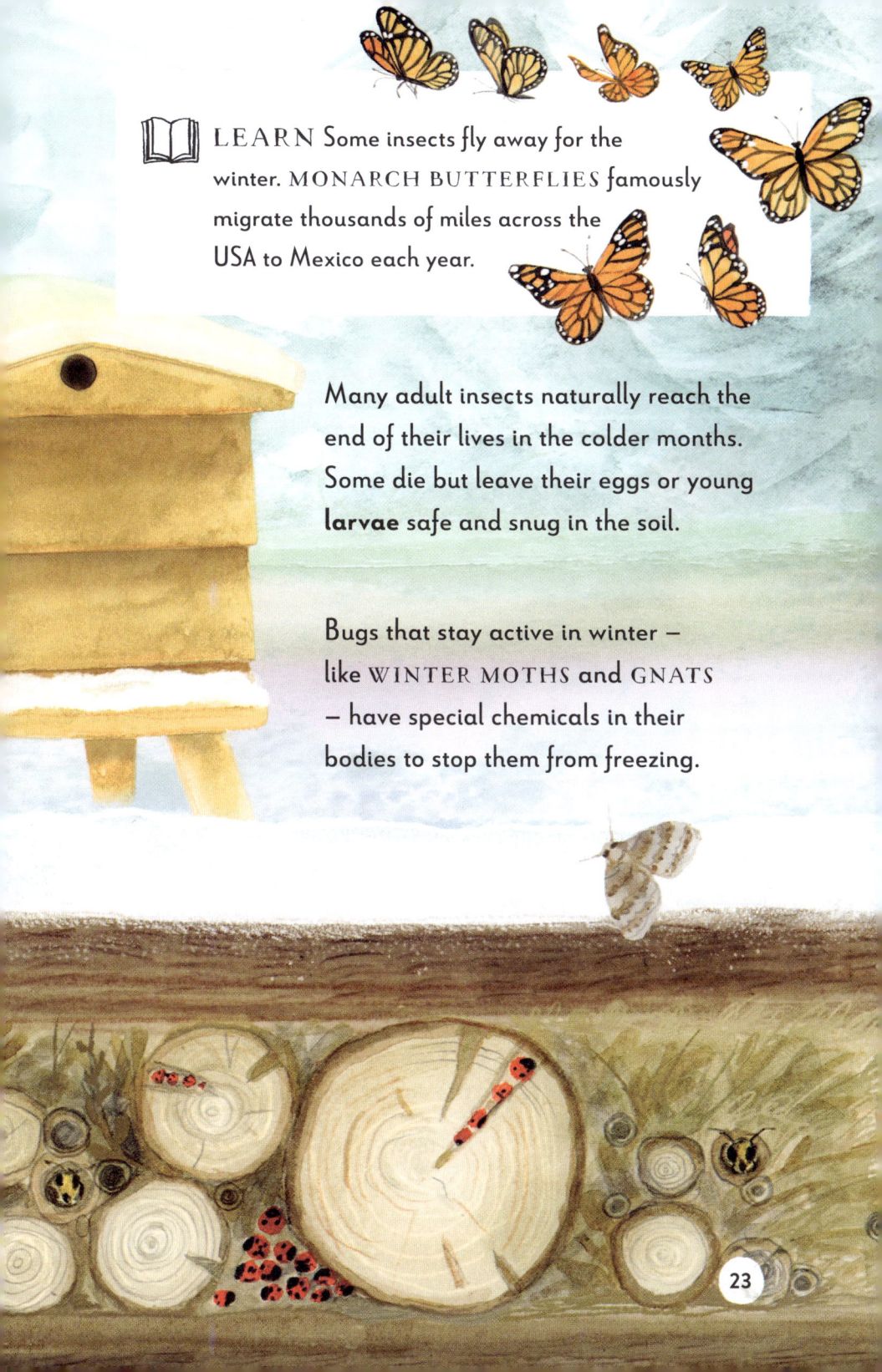

📖 **LEARN** Some insects fly away for the winter. **MONARCH BUTTERFLIES** famously migrate thousands of miles across the USA to Mexico each year.

Many adult insects naturally reach the end of their lives in the colder months. Some die but leave their eggs or young **larvae** safe and snug in the soil.

Bugs that stay active in winter — like **WINTER MOTHS** and **GNATS** — have special chemicals in their bodies to stop them from freezing.

bare branches

Why trees lose their leaves

As the weather gets colder, notice how the trees are changing...

Deciduous trees – such as ASH, BEECH, SILVER BIRCH, OAK and MAPLE – shed their shimmering golden, red and copper leaves every year in autumn.

As many animals keep warm in winter by growing extra-thick coats, these trees look cold and bare by comparison!

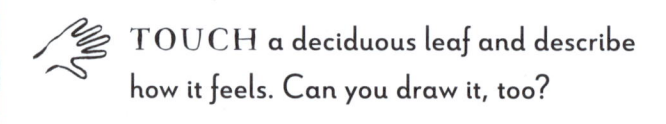

> TOUCH a deciduous leaf and describe how it feels. Can you draw it, too?

LISTEN Can you hear branches creaking in the wind?

Deciduous trees and shrubs lose their leaves to save energy and make them less likely to blow over in the windy winter months.

The fallen leaves turn into **leaf mulch**, which feeds worms and other bugs, and gives **nutrients** back to the soil as the fragments dissolve into the earth. These nutrients provide valuable food for plants, including the trees they came from.

When spring arrives, the trees are ready to grow new shoots and buds again!

forever green

Trees that keep their leaves

Not all trees lose their leaves in winter. **Evergreen trees** stay green all year long!

Evergreens — such as PINE, YEW and HOLLY, or splendid RHODODENDRON bushes — have very different leaves to their deciduous relatives.

Next time you go for a walk, find an evergreen shrub or tree and look at its leaves. What do they look like?

LEARN Berries are welcome food for many animals in winter. When they poop out the pips, they spread the seeds of new plants and trees!

👃 SMELL Trees with needles, such as pine, spruce and fir, often have a fresh scent. What does the smell remind you of?

Evergreen foliage is often a dark shade of green with tough, waxy leaves, which are good for keeping the cold out.

Their leaf shape can be pointed, prickly or sharp, which makes them less appetising for animals to munch on. Some evergreen trees and shrubs produce bright berries to entice birds and other animals instead. But most of these berries are poisonous to humans.

We call some thin, pointy, evergreen leaves 'needles'. Can you guess why?

winter leaves

How to identify evergreen trees

HOLLY
- Dark green, shiny leaves
- Younger trees have spiky leaves, but old trees have smooth leaves.
- Bright red berries in winter

SPRUCE
- Stiff, pointy needles
- Needles grow individually around the branch.
- Long, scaly cones hang down from the branch.

LEARN Holly has prickly leaves to stop animals like deer from nibbling its branches.

👁 **LOOK** Trees with needles can be hard to tell apart at first glance, so look closely.

PINE
- Long, thin needles
- Needles grow in groups of 2 to 5 from a single point on the branch.
- Woody cones hang from the branch.

YEW
- Flat needles with pointed tips
- Needles are dark green on top and lighter underneath.
- Needles grow in two rows on either side of the branch.

frozen gems

Make your own ice ornaments

Make a bare tree even more beautiful by creating some icy decorations to hang on it.

YOU WILL NEED:
- string
- scissors
- containers — such as small dishes, ice cube trays and recycled plastic pots
- natural decorations — such as leaves, berries, nuts and seeds
- water

1. Make loops to hang your ornaments by cutting lengths of string and knotting the ends together.

2. Place a loop into each container, leaving enough string sticking out to hang on a tree later.

3. Arrange your natural decorations inside your containers. Place a few on top of each string to weigh it down.

4. Carefully fill your containers with water.

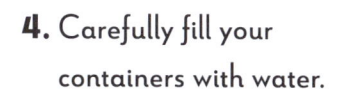

LOOK How long does it take your ornaments to melt? Hours? Days? Weeks?

5. If it's cold enough, leave the containers outside overnight to freeze. Otherwise, put them in the freezer.

6. Once frozen, pop your ornaments out of their containers and use them to decorate a tree.

RESPECT NATURE Look for materials that have fallen to the ground instead of picking or cutting them from plants. Once your decorations have melted, don't forget to collect the pieces of string.

freezing
Jack Frost

Chilly winter mornings

On crisp winter mornings, every surface and each leaf, twig and blade of grass is dressed in tiny, diamond-like ice crystals. This is **frost**. It forms when water in the air, called water vapour, lands on a cold surface and freezes.

Wake up early for a chance to catch frost sparkling in the tender sunshine. Wrap up warm and off you go for an adventure outdoors. Remember to take a grown-up with you!

Walk across sparkling paths and pavements. Stomp over frost-crisp grass patches, leaving footprints as you go. Find a frozen puddle and slide across it! Can you break the ice with your boot?

SMELL Even on a frosty morning, the cold air is full of scents. What can you smell on a cold winter's day?

TOUCH Feel the cool air and the warm sun on your face.

LISTEN What can you hear?

When water cools down to 0°C or lower, it turns to ice. Perfect sheets of smooth, slippery ice can form on the surface of puddles and ponds. Sometimes whole lakes will freeze over if it gets really cold outside!

WATCH OUT for slippery ice patches on paths and pavements. Don't walk on frozen ponds or lakes.

life under the ice

What happens to pond life?

Have you ever wondered what happens to fish or frogs when their homes freeze over?

Where do lake, loch, pool and pond-dwellers go and how do they survive the freeze?

Believe it or not, a layer of ice actually helps to keep the water below warmer, providing shelter from the weather above. Even though the water at the bottom is still very cold, it is just warm enough for the animals and plants that live there to survive.

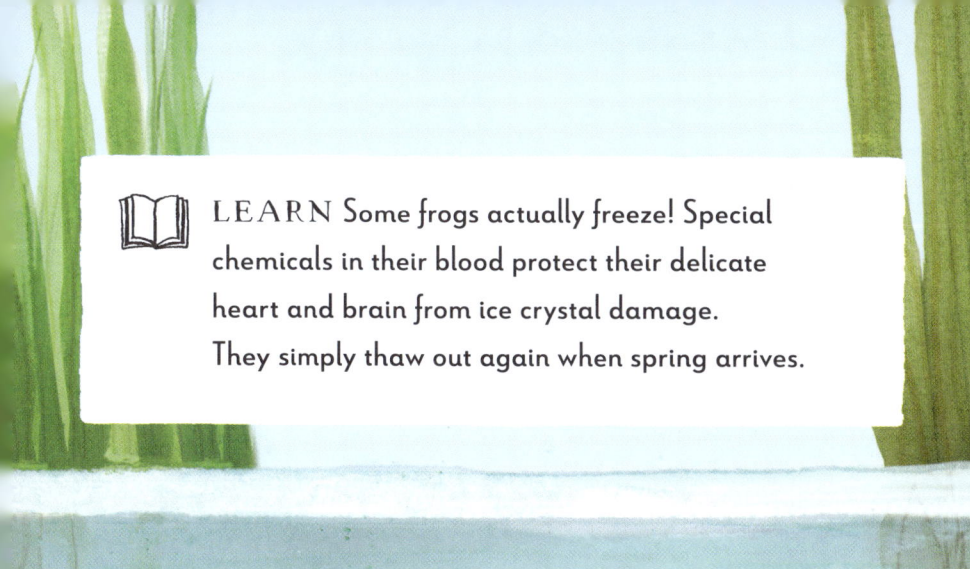

📖 **LEARN** Some frogs actually freeze! Special chemicals in their blood protect their delicate heart and brain from ice crystal damage. They simply thaw out again when spring arrives.

Most **aquatic** INSECTS simply sink to the bottom, where the water is warmest. There they wait patiently in the mud for spring to arrive.

Some FROGS dig into the soft, mushy pond bed and doze through winter. Frogs can breathe through their skin, and by keeping still they use very little energy. Other frogs will leave the pond before it freezes to find a log to rest beneath, or a cosy compost heap or protective mound of mulch to snuggle in.

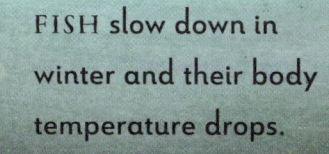

FISH slow down in winter and their body temperature drops.

a warming winter soup

To sip from a mug

There is nothing quite as comforting on a cold day as a mug of warming, homemade soup. Many tasty root vegetables — such as carrots, potatoes, parsnips, beetroot and turnips — grow in winter, snug in the soil.

INGREDIENTS:

- 2 tbsp olive oil or melted butter
- 1 large onion (chopped)
- 2 sticks of celery (finely chopped)
- 3 carrots (peeled and chopped)
- 1 potato (peeled and chopped)
- 1 litre of vegetable stock
- 2 bay leaves
- salt and pepper, to taste

optional (for extra sweetness):
- 1 parsnip, small squash or sweet potato — peeled and chopped

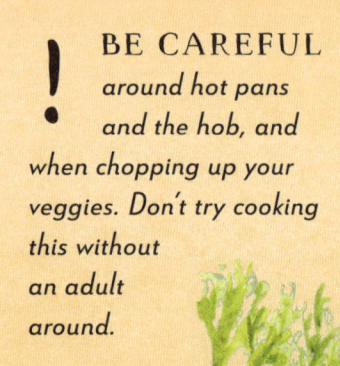

! BE CAREFUL around hot pans and the hob, and when chopping up your veggies. Don't try cooking this without an adult around.

1. Warm the oil or butter in a large, heavy-bottomed saucepan.

2. Add the chopped onion and celery to the pan and gently cook until completely soft.

3. Add the chopped carrots, potato and any other vegetables you are using and cook for about 5 minutes.

4. Pour in the stock and add the bay leaves.

5. Let all the ingredients simmer until totally tender. This will take around 25 minutes, perhaps longer, depending on your choice of veggies.

6. Remove the bay leaves before squashing the vegetables with a potato masher — or whizz everything up in a blender for a smoother soup.

7. Taste your soup and add salt and pepper if needed.

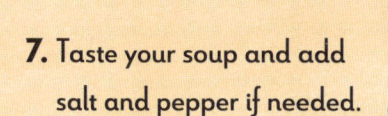

party time for polar bears

A song to sing on a winter walk

Unless you live in the Arctic, you're unlikely to come across a polar bear on your winter's day walk. But just imagine...

(Sing to the tune of *The Teddy Bears' Picnic**)

If you go onto the ice today
you're in for a big surprise.
If you go onto the ice today
you'll never believe your eyes...
For lots of bears with raggedy fur
are standing round and causing a stir –
today's the day the polar bears
have their party!

CHORUS:
Party time for polar bears!
The furry polar bears are dancing
upon the ice today.
See them play – they have no cares!
And watch them party on their holiday...

See them skiing down the slopes,
and skipping over ropes,
play records and dance on chairs!
And after eating dishes of fishes
they tiptoe back to bed
along the cool, frosty, iceberg stairs!

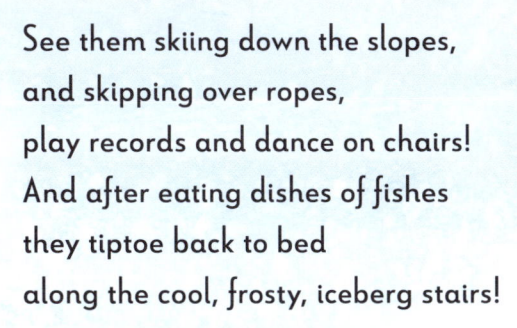

Every polar bear wears a coat
and even a winter hat.
There's music playing and treats to eat,
now what do you think of that?
Below the snow where nobody goes,
they snuggle up and wiggle their toes,
But hey today the polar bears
have their party!

REPEAT CHORUS

Watch them swimming in the sea –
too cold for you and me!
But not for the polar bears...
And after eating dishes of fishes
they tiptoe back to bed
because they're tired little polar bears!

(*The Teddy Bears' Picnic, original lyrics by Jimmy Kennedy and music by John Walter Bratton)

frosty feathers

What do birds do in winter?

Next time you go out for a chilly winter walk, stop and listen. Can you hear any birdsong? Birds sing all year round but in winter the air is not quite as full of bird sounds as other seasons.

Still, if you open your ears you might hear the bright-breasted ROBIN singing his clear, vibrant song or the loud, high-pitched whistles of a tiny WREN!

Winter is a challenging time for birds. The ground becomes hard in the cold, which makes it more difficult to peck for worms and grubs, and there are far fewer insects to be found. Although some trees and bushes glow with jewel-like berries for birds to eat, there is much less food to go around than in warmer months.

Some birds leave their homes and fly away to spend winter in warmer countries where there is more food to be had. This is called **migration**.

Hardy birds that stay behind have special tricks to stay warm in the cold. Have you noticed some birds looking particularly fluffy? That's because they puff out their feathers to trap warm air around their bodies. Many birds also huddle together to share each other's body heat.

LEARN The only bird known to hibernate is the POORWILL. This North American bird is perfectly **camouflaged** for hiding amongst rocks and leaves, where it rests for much of the winter.

lending birds a helping hand

How to help birds in winter

When the ground hardens and food is scarce, when trees are bare and puddles transform into mini ice rinks... how do birds get food to eat? Where do they shelter from the rain and sleet?

You don't need to have a garden to help birds in winter — a windowsill with space for a tray will do. Or find a nearby tree with a branch to hang a birdfeeder. All you need is a safe space that clever cats and greedy squirrels can't reach!

LOOK How many birds can you see? Can you identify them?

! **BE SAFE** You should always wear rubber gloves when cleaning feeders or trays and wash your hands thoroughly afterwards.

A mix of seeds, peanuts, dry oats and fatty suet makes an excellent meal for birds. You could also add some chopped fruit as an extra-tasty treat.

When ponds and puddles freeze over, it can be hard for birds to find water to drink. Leave out a shallow dish of clean water where they can have a drink or take a bath.

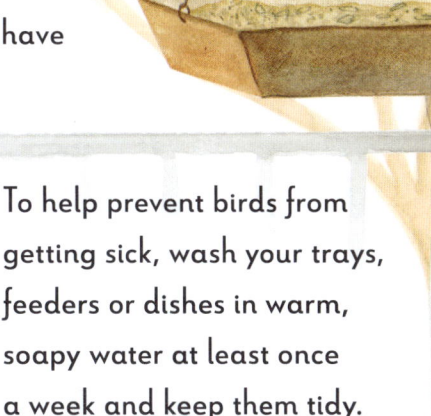

To help prevent birds from getting sick, wash your trays, feeders or dishes in warm, soapy water at least once a week and keep them tidy. Refresh food and water daily.

Now you can sit back and watch your feathered friends. Try not to disturb them!

cold winds blow

Make your own winter wind chimes

As winter winds whip and whirl, try your hand at making some wind chimes from materials you can find on a walk.

YOU WILL NEED:
- sticks and twigs
- pine cones
- string
- scissors

1. Pick a nice sturdy stick that you'd like to hang your chimes from.

2. Select smaller sticks or twigs to use as chimes, snapping them to size if you need to.

3. Tie a piece of string around one end of each stick and around the middle of your pine cones.

TIP *There are lots of other things you could use as chimes! Shells, nuts and pebbles make good noises, and feathers or leaves would look lovely.*

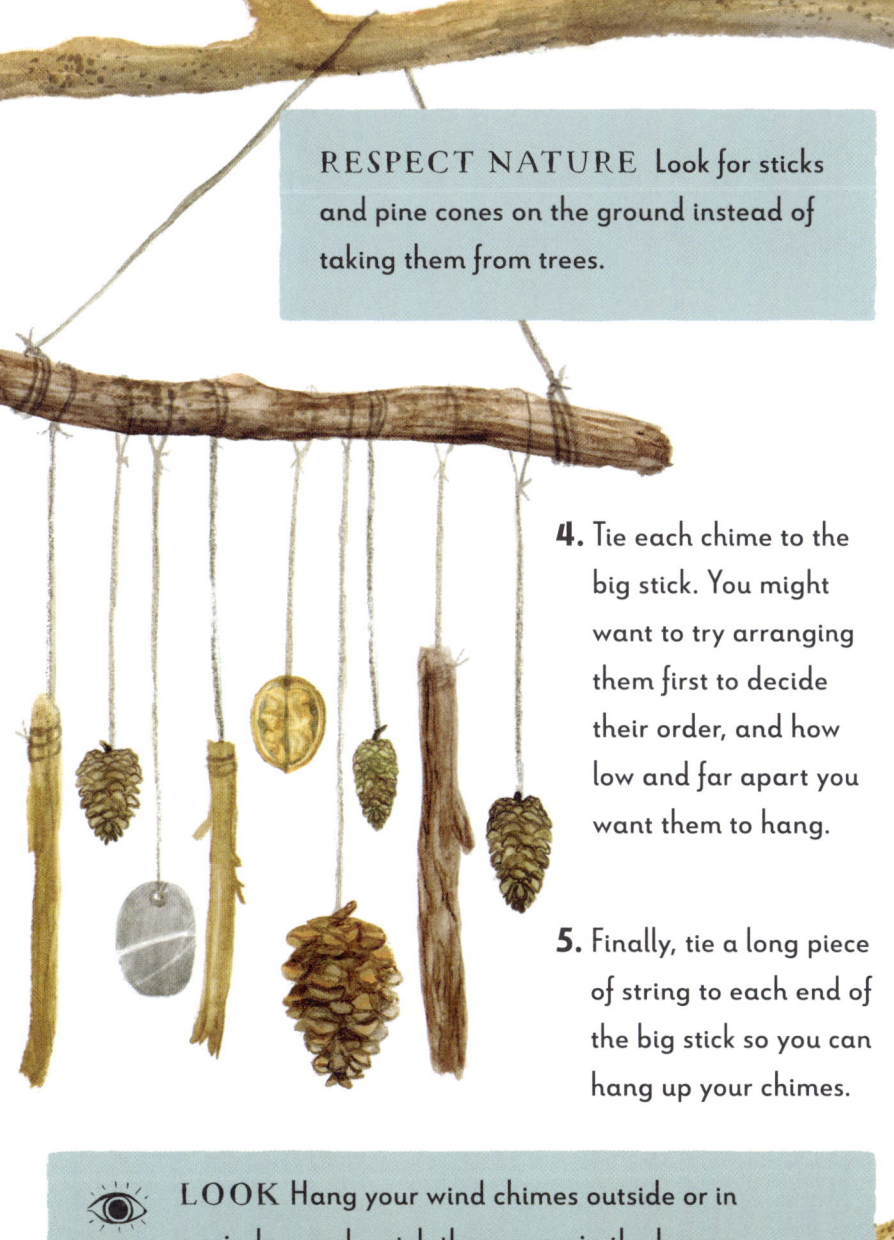

RESPECT NATURE Look for sticks and pine cones on the ground instead of taking them from trees.

4. Tie each chime to the big stick. You might want to try arranging them first to decide their order, and how low and far apart you want them to hang.

5. Finally, tie a long piece of string to each end of the big stick so you can hang up your chimes.

LOOK Hang your wind chimes outside or in a window and watch them sway in the breeze.

LISTEN to the wind and the sound your chimes make as they knock into each other.

starry, starry night

All eyes on the winter skies

Long winter nights are the perfect time for stargazing. The stars appear brighter because the cool air of winter is clearer than warm, hazy summer air.

It's easier to see stars in the countryside, where there is less **artificial light** from buildings, street lamps and vehicles. Towns and cities are full of light at night, which makes it harder to see the stars. But you should still be able to stargaze there if you can find a good spot.

For the best view wherever you live, look for a high place where you can easily see the sky. This could be the top of a hill or a balcony in a tall building. Even a skylight can offer a good view.

Pick a cloudless night when no rain is forecast. If you're going outside, wear your warmest coat, hat and gloves, and don't forget to go with a grown-up!

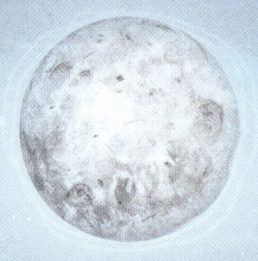

You want it to be as dark as possible, so once you've found a good spot, put away phones and torches, and allow your eyes to adjust to the dark. If you're indoors or in your garden, turn off all the lights in your home.

LOOK UP and see the universe unfolding above like a star-spangled canopy of inky-black.

Can you see the moon?
How many stars do you think there are?
Could you count them all?
Which is the brightest star you can see?

pictures in the sky

How to identify constellations

If you look closely at the stars, patterns might start to emerge. Imagine drawing a line between stars, like a dot-to-dot puzzle. What shapes could you make?

Groups of stars that form a shape or a pattern are called **constellations**. Here are a few to look out for in the winter sky:

ORION (THE HUNTER)

- Looks a bit like a hunter holding a sword and shield (or you might think it looks more like a bow and arrow).
- First, look for three bright stars close together in a line. That's 'Orion's Belt'.

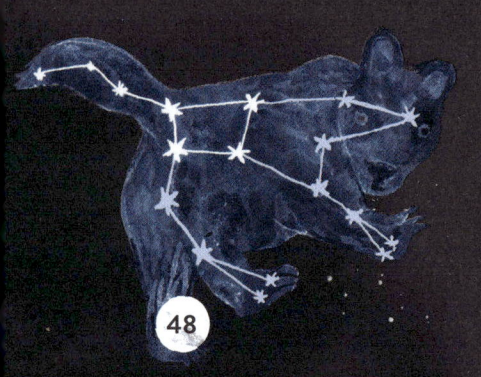

URSA MAJOR (THE GREAT BEAR)

- Looks a bit like a bear.
- It contains a smaller pattern known as 'The Plough' or 'The Big Dipper', which looks like a saucepan. Look for this first as it's easiest to spot.

TIPS
- The way you're facing will affect which constellations you can see and which way up they appear, so look all around you!
- Binoculars will give you a clearer view, if you have a pair.

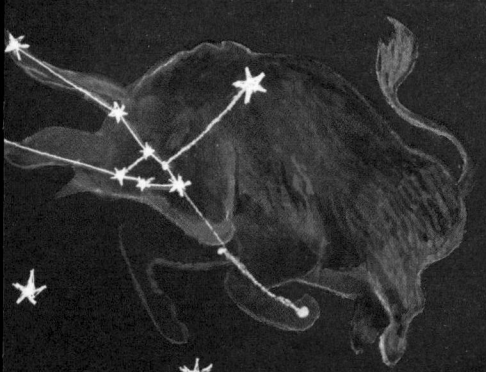

TAURUS (THE BULL)
- Looks like the head and chest of a bull with very long horns.
- Can be found just to the right of Orion.

GEMINI (THE TWINS)
- Looks like two stick people holding hands.
- The brightest stars are the two heads, which are named Castor and Pollux after twins from Greek mythology.

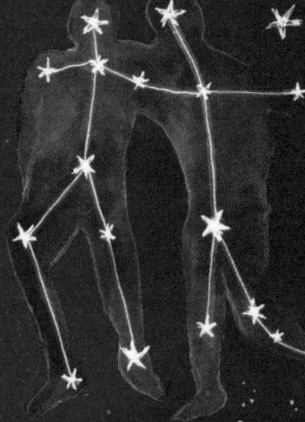

LOOK Don't worry if you can't find any constellations — it's just as fun to make up your own! What shapes can you see? What would you name them?

mini night sky

Make your own constellation lantern

Light up the long nights with your own mini constellations!

YOU WILL NEED:

- a glass jar (remove any labels)
- kitchen foil
- scissors
- a sharp pencil or cocktail stick
- a ball of sticky tack or an eraser
- an LED tealight

1. Cut a piece of foil so it is just long enough to wrap around your jar.

2. Cut the foil again so it is roughly the same height as the distance between the bottom and neck of the jar. Then lay your foil sheet out flat.

3. Now it's time for your stars! Make holes by carefully poking the tip of a sharp pencil or cocktail stick through the foil into a ball of sticky tack or an eraser.

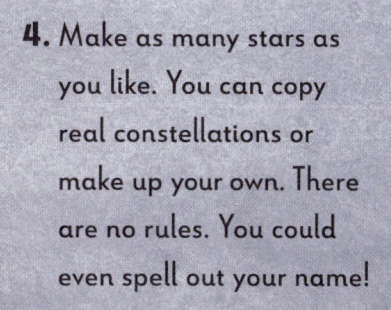

4. Make as many stars as you like. You can copy real constellations or make up your own. There are no rules. You could even spell out your name!

TIP *If you like, you can plan out your constellations by drawing onto the back of the foil with a marker pen.*

5. When you've finished your constellations, carefully roll up the foil into a tube shape so you can fit it into the jar. Then unwind the foil and push it out so it fits up against the inner sides of the jar. You may need to use a pencil or the back of a spoon to help you smooth it out.

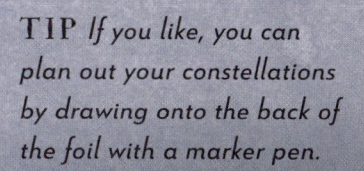

6. Pop your tealight into the jar, turn off the lights, and enjoy your glowing constellations!

treasure hunt

Searching for signs of winter

There are many treasures waiting to be found in winter. Next time you plan a trip to the park, woods or a green space near where you live, look out for the following...

A BIRD to hear. Listen to their song. Can you identify them?

Bright BERRIES to draw. Describe their branch. Do you know their name?

A STONE to hold. How does it feel? Rough or smooth?

An ICY PUDDLE to step on. What sound does the ice make as it breaks?

TIP *look out for flowers that grow in winter, such as* HELLEBORES *and* SNOWDROPS. *Not many flowers grow in winter, so they are extra special!*

PINE NEEDLES to sniff. What does the smell remind you of?

A FEATHER to feel. Is it soft? Which bird did it come from?

PAW PRINTS to spot. Who made them? Where do they lead?

A TWIG to snap. What tree is it from? Where are its leaves?

A FLOWER to see. What colour is it? Can you draw it?

An evergreen LEAF to draw. What shape is it? What colour is it?

winter's bone

A poem to read on a chilly day

I stare across the frozen ground,
the trees are bare, the earth is grey,
the fallen leaves have blown away
but still are treasures to be found...

The glassy ice upon the pond,
the sparkling white of frosty grass,
the gentle sunshine as we pass,
the chilly scent of snow beyond...

Look! These jewels upon the tree
are winterberries, ruby red,
that all the birds can eat (instead
of human folk, like you and me).

The quiet hush of icy air
as stars begin to prick the sky,
and soon the moon will rise up high
to light the nightly creatures there...

📖 **LEARN** 'Winter's bone' comes from an old Appalachian expression, 'like a dog digging after a winter's bone' – meaning someone who is searching for something and won't give up.

Until the sound of silence brings
a crack, a snap, a distant howl,
and suddenly a wide-eyed owl
alights like mist on feathered wings...

♡ While winter reigns upon her throne,
the garden rests and all along
the robin sings his cheery song
to make the earth feel less alone...

☆ For all of nature understands
that winter is the time to slow,
to sleep and wait awhile to grow
once more upon the fields and lands.

But even in the cold and rain,
the world keeps turning round and round
while solid stays the frozen ground
until the spring awakes again.

go prepared

Tips for the outdoors

What to pack
The weather can be very cold and wet so it's important to dress properly to stay warm and dry.

Top tips:
- Wear two pairs of socks to keep your toes toasty and pack a spare pair in case you get soggy!
- Wear plenty of layers and pack extra jumpers or fleeces so that you can easily take layers off if you're warm or put more on if you're cold.

Raincoat

Thermal top and trousers (to wear under your clothes)

Waterproof trousers or dungarees

Wellies or outdoor boots

Jumper or fleece

Stay safe

- Never touch or pick plants without permission from an adult.
- **Foraging** for food can be fun, but don't eat anything you find outdoors unless an adult tells you it's safe.
- Make sure an adult always knows where you are and don't wander off alone.
- Be careful near ponds, rivers and lakes – especially if they are frozen. Don't go in the water without an adult nearby and never walk on frozen ponds or lakes.
- Ice and snow can make the ground very slippery so take care and look where you're stepping.

Water bottle

Snacks

Woolly hat

Rucksack

Scarf

Gloves

Notebook and pencil

Respect wildlife

- Try to leave nature as you found it.
- Put your litter in a bin, or take it home with you.
- Try not to disturb wild animals.

field notes

Recording winter's changes

Keeping a nature journal or scrapbook is a fun and creative way to appreciate nature and track the changing seasons.

Here are some ideas to get you started:

- Draw and paint.
- Press leaves, flowers and seeds between journal pages.
- Make rubbings — leaves, bark and rocks work well!
- Write your own winter poems and stories.
- Keep a weather diary to track changes.
- Include photographs you've taken in nature.
  - Pick a tree and record how it changes over time. How and when do its leaves change? Or do they stay the same?
    - Make a note of the animals and plants you spot. Can you identify them all?
    - Once you've identified something, keep a tally of how many you see.

Observation notes

Here are some questions to ask yourself when you spot an animal or plant:

1. What colour is it?

2. What shape and size is it?

3. What would it feel like to touch?

4. Does it have a smell?

5. What sound does it make?

winter words

aquatic
Something that lives or grows in or near to water.

artificial light
Light that is produced by sources made by humans, such as electric torches, lamps or streetlights.

camouflaged
When something looks like its surroundings in order to blend in or hide.

constellations
Groups of stars that appear to form a particular pattern or shape.

deciduous trees
Trees that shed their leaves in autumn.

diapause
A state some animals go into over winter, where they stop moving, growing and ageing.

equator
An imaginary line drawn around the middle of the Earth.

equinox
An event that happens twice a year when day and night are the same length.

evergreen trees
Trees that keep their leaves all year round.

foraging
When a person or animal searches for food in the wild.

frost
A layer of ice crystals formed when water vapour in the air lands and freezes on a cold surface.

hibernation
A state of deep sleep or rest that some animals go into over winter to keep warm and save energy.

larvae
Young insects, in the stage before they change into their adult form.

leaf mulch
A layer of fallen leaves that protects and feeds the soil as it rots down.

metabolism
The processes in a body that turn food into energy.

migration
When a group of animals travels from one place to another at certain times of year.

northern hemisphere
The half of Earth that is north of the equator.

nutrients
Substances that give energy to living things that consume them.

paw pad
A soft area on the bottom of an animal's paw.

southern hemisphere
The half of Earth that is south of the equator.

torpor
A state similar to hibernation that some animals go into over winter. They spend most of the time resting, but may occasionally get up to find food.

webbed feet
Feet with toes joined together by skin. Animals such as water birds and frogs have webbed feet to help them move through water.

winter solstice
The shortest day of the year, when Earth is tilted furthest away from the sun.

index

animal tracks 16–17
artificial light 46
ash trees 24

badgers 18
bats 19
bears 19, 38–39, 48
bedtime story 20–21
beech trees 24
bees 22
berries 26, 27, 28, 30, 40, 52
birds 17, 40–41, 42–43, 52
butterflies 22, 23

camouflage 41, 60
constellation lanterns 50–51
constellations 48–49

deciduous trees 24–25, 60
deer 16
diapause 22, 60
dormice 19

equator 13, 60
evergreen trees 26–27, 28–29, 53, 60

field notes 58–59
fir trees 27

fish 34, 35
flowers 53, 58
foxes 16
frogs 34, 35
frost 32–33, 40

gnats 23

hedgehogs 19
hellebores 53
hibernation 18–19, 41
holly trees 26, 28

ice crystals 14, 32
ice ornaments 30–31
insects 22–23, 35

ladybirds 22
larvae 23, 61
leaf mulch 25, 61
leaves 24–25, 26–27, 28–29, 30, 53, 58
listen 8, 11, 15, 22, 25, 33, 40, 45, 52
lizards 18
look 8, 17, 29, 31, 42, 45, 47, 49, 51, 54

maple trees 24
metabolism 18, 61
migration 23, 41, 61
moon 47
monarch butterflies 23

newts 18
night 9, 13, 46–47
northern hemisphere 13, 61
nutrients 25, 61

oak trees 24

paw prints 16–17, 53
pine cones 44
pine needles 53
pine trees 26, 27, 29
poems 10–11, 38–39, 54–55
polar bears 38–39
ponds 33, 34–35, 57
poorwill 41
puddles 32, 33, 52

rabbits 17
rhododendron 26
robins 17, 40

silver birch trees 24
smell 8, 27, 33, 53

snakes 18
snow 14–15, 16–17, 57
snowdrops 53
snowflakes 14, 15
solstice 13
sounds 8, 40
soup 36–37
southern hemisphere 13, 61
spruce trees 27, 28
squirrels 17
stars 46–47, 48–49, 50–51, 60

taste 8, 15, 37
tips for outdoors 56–57
toads 18
torpor 18, 61
touch 8, 15, 33
treasure hunt 52–53
trees 8, 9, 24–25, 26–27, 28–29, 53

water vapour 32
webbed feet 17, 61
wind chimes 44–45
winter moths 23
wrens 40

yew trees 26, 29

GABBY DAWNAY

Gabby is the award-winning author of over 30 books for children, poet-in-residence at children's art and science magazine *OKIDO* and a scriptwriter for children's television.

DORIEN BROUWERS

Dorien is an award-winning illustrator and author. She started writing and illustrating picture books as a gift for her son.

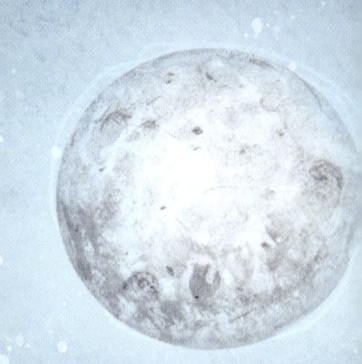